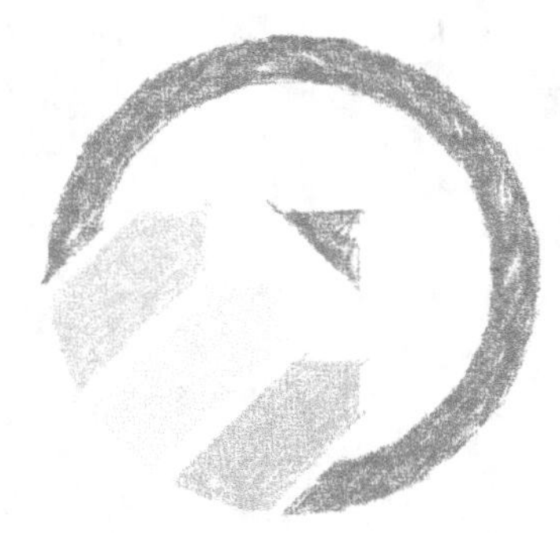

Color Chart
LOG BOOK

This book belongs to:

How to Use This Book

This notebook is a handy way to keep track of your art supplies and create a color reference.

- Color charts can be created based upon the type of media, product brands, hues or even based upon seasons or moods.
- For best results, use a piece of cardstock between your pages when creating your swatches to help prevent bleed through.

Chart Name _____________________ Brand/Medium:__________

Chart Name _______________________ Brand/Medium:__________

Chart Name ________________________ Brand/Medium:__________

Chart Name _______________________ Brand/Medium:__________

Chart Name ________________________ Brand/Medium:__________

Chart Name _____________________ Brand/Medium:__________

Chart Name _______________________ Brand/Medium:___________

Chart Name ________________________ Brand/Medium:__________

Chart Name ______________________ Brand/Medium:__________

Chart Name ____________________________ Brand/Medium:__________

Chart Name ______________________ Brand/Medium:_________

Chart Name _____________________ Brand/Medium:__________

Chart Name _____________________________ Brand/Medium:__________

Chart Name _____________________ Brand/Medium:_________

Chart Name ______________________ Brand/Medium:_________

Chart Name _____________________ Brand/Medium:__________

Chart Name ______________________ Brand/Medium:__________

Chart Name _____________________ Brand/Medium:__________

Chart Name ________________________ Brand/Medium:_________

Chart Name _______________________ Brand/Medium:__________

Chart Name _______________________ Brand/Medium:___________

Chart Name _______________________ Brand/Medium:__________

Chart Name _______________________ Brand/Medium:__________

Chart Name ___________________________ Brand/Medium:___________

Chart Name _____________________ Brand/Medium:__________

Chart Name ______________________ Brand/Medium:__________

Chart Name _______________________ Brand/Medium:__________

Chart Name _____________________ Brand/Medium:__________

Chart Name _______________________ Brand/Medium:__________

Chart Name _____________________ Brand/Medium:__________

Chart Name ________________________ Brand/Medium:__________

Chart Name ___________________________ Brand/Medium:__________

Chart Name _____________________________ Brand/Medium:___________

Chart Name _______________________ Brand/Medium:__________

Chart Name ______________________________ Brand/Medium:__________

Chart Name _______________________ Brand/Medium:___________

Chart Name _______________________ Brand/Medium:__________

Chart Name _______________________ Brand/Medium:_________

Chart Name _____________________ Brand/Medium:__________

Chart Name _______________________ Brand/Medium:_________

Chart Name _______________________ Brand/Medium:___________

Chart Name ___________________________ Brand/Medium:___________

Chart Name ______________________ Brand/Medium:_________

Chart Name _____________________ Brand/Medium:_________

Chart Name _____________________ Brand/Medium:__________

Chart Name ______________________ Brand/Medium:_________

Chart Name _____________________ Brand/Medium:_________